ON THE WAY HOME

TOM HUNTER

Cover by Anya Kelleye Designs
Anyakelleye.com

Edited and Formatted by
Brackish Publishing
brackishpublishing.com

FOREWORD

As an old saying goes, there is nothing certain in life, except death and taxes. None of us know what will happen even a moment from now, much less the broader future and therein lies the rub. We plan, we forecast and we analyze, but, ultimately, we make decisions with some degree of unknown and imperfect information. We press on anyway because we must. Otherwise, we would be paralyzed.

So, within each imperfect daily decision, there is, inevitably, some doubt. The same can apply to our spiritual lives and development; why would we expect our spiritual lives to be different?

Moses did not feel he was up to the task of leading Israel out of Egypt. Jonah tried to run away until God used a great fish to truly get his attention. Elijah, despite a great victory, became despondent and wanted to die. Sarah did not believe she would have a child in her old age. In Psalm 22, even David, a man reputed to have held a special place in God's heart, laments, "My God, my God, why have you forsaken me?" God had not forsaken, or abandoned, David, and we, thousands of years later, see how the relationship between God and David played out. David, distressed by events and circumstances, had moments of doubt, as well as moments of confidence and certainty.

From the cross, Jesus Christ also uttered those same words from Psalm 22. Although we cannot know or explain how or why Jesus Christ uttered those words, could even He have had a moment of doubt? He was God incarnate, but He was also a man—in all ways.

So, here we are—mere mortals—simultaneously living earthly and spiritual lives and in both, I submit, doubt abounds. There is no way around it. Even the best of men and women have their doubts, right? It is enough to know the narrow path that leads to heaven, even with setbacks, even with potholes of doubt, is the right way and is a path of increasing faith and assurance of salvation.

DEDICATION

There are so many to whom I could dedicate this collection of poems. There is my partner, my wife, Carole, who gave me nothing but encouragement throughout this project. There are the faithful members of my Sunday School class, who inspired me to look inward, dig deeper and allow the Holy Spirit to put words on my paper. There are my two sons, Matthew and Harrison, who have always been my great joy, who have matured into good Christian husbands and fathers and who, in so doing, have made me so proud. And, there is that long line, that legion of Christians, who have made indelible marks and contributions to my life and who lovingly helped me find Jesus, and myself, along the way.

But, notwithstanding all of those mentioned above, I have chosen to dedicate this book to my precious grandchildren: Griffin, Huck, Brighton, Holden, Kipp, and Bell. Today, they are all very young and they have their entire lives ahead of them. It is my hope that someday, perhaps, when I am but a dim and distant memory for them, they will read what the Holy Spirit has inspired me to write and thereby gain a better understanding of who I was and of who I am. I am a soul and a spirit, who will live forever in Heaven with Jesus Christ, my Lord, and my fervent prayer is that they will join me one day where I am.

WAITING

I thought myself a real Renaissance man.
I was sophisticated, smart, well-spoken and tanned,
Worldly, wealthy, aloof and fit,
One hundred percent on top of "it".

I had no help, I did it all.
Whether way out in front or against the wall,
Made some winners out of losing hands,
Revised every day my well-thought plans.

I cracked so many—more than a few—
The numbskulls who just wouldn't do.
And each one who said, "There's more out there,"
Got a condescending and icy stare.

I was demanding and cautious and calm—never rash,
I scanned what I read like one picks through the trash.
I even heard a church sermon once, so I think,
And it didn't impress; it did not make me blink.

A God out there in "somewhere land"?

I hadn't seen His face or held His hand.
I thought Him a figment to soothe the hearts,
Of losers who dined on bits and parts.

Then my fortunes changed, my world imploded,
My wisdom was rocked, it faltered, eroded.
I fell among those I had pitied, detested,
Those who toiled with joy and, though struggling, rested.

Peace in the God I'd dismissed as myth?
They'd put life in perspective, found substance, pith,
On this orb, these few said, we must love one another,
To prepare us for life in a new world, another.

They made the impression, I'm happy to say,
I'm more thankful and honest and humble today.
And with Christ at the helm, I'm not worried the path,
He shields my weak spirit from justice and wrath.

Why did I not fathom God's love way back when?
Why was I so blinded by trinkets and sin?
From the first light of dawn those who sought God have
found,
He's been eagerly waiting; He's been hanging around.

Truth always endures, while lies fade away,
And the legion of saints marching down to this day,
Have given fair warning to each modern thinker,
Swallow not the deception, not hook, line and sinker.

ON THE NUCLEOTIDE?

Am I alone in my struggle in this sea called mankind?
In the vastness of time is there meaning to find?
Am I a small, nameless ant buried deep in a hill,
Whose dull days are numbered 'til I'm cold and I'm still?
Or, is there something else, something more, to delight and to thrill?
My brain's lobes debate and they may always will.

Is it the organic molecule on a small helix double,
Inside of my cells causing tension and trouble?
Does it make me unique and so different from others,
Nature/nurture, no matter—from my sisters and brothers?
Am I joined to one greater, on the far side of sight,
I wonder when I drift between dreams in the night.

Logic and reason and science and sense,
With space and with time never-ending, immense.
I can't articulate questions, it's malicious and cruel,
When I try to employ just a small "what-if" tool.
My little brain screams, "When I'm dead, I am dead!"
But still I must question what my little brain said.

If there's nothing more to my essence, when my dim lights
go out,
When my lungs exhale feebly to end this short bout,
If I'm just treading water, while I play out my time,
Why am I so troubled, if there's no reason or rhyme?
For if death is so settled, why waste even a moment,
Why question, why query, why give way to the torment?

Why have all those before me—from the true dawn of man,
Asked that question? Is it coded on my two-helix strand?
And if the question is there, there's a good purpose, right,
Not just fodder for struggle, when I can't sleep at night.
If the question's there, maybe the answer's there, too,
Awaiting some researcher's litmus or brew!

If the answer-thing's hiding, if it's there in plain sight,
Behind some nucleoli and just to the right,
Then I can quit with my worry about the grand scheme of
things,
I can sleep well at night with the dust Sandman brings.
Perhaps some nucleotide plays a really BIG role,
Just a feature passed down to all—maybe a... soul?

THE PATH

There was a season, a day, a time,
When life seemed simple and so sublime.
When I was so blind, so deaf, so dumb,
When just one mattered; I was that one.

With meaningless motions my senses were numbed,
No winners or losers in a game, zero sum.
I existed, not living, with no passion, no flame,
In a mansion of toys with a gold-plated name.

Others thought me a warrior from the scalps on my belt,
No one bothered to ask what I thought, how I felt.
I had a smooth, slick façade made of vinyl veneer,
Little stuck or got through, especially cheer.

I had all; I had nothing, from two points of view,
I was lighter than air; I was thicker than stew,
I was missing in action; I was right in the fray,
But my heart had a hole; I was slipping away.

Why did I feel empty? Why did I feel sad?

I grew up in a home with a great mom and dad!
Was there more to this life than just counting the days?
Was there magic, excitement, something meant to amaze?

Then, one day I found "it" (or it came and found me),
Some words I had heard that turned out to be key,
And all of the emptiness, all the pain and the wrath,
Began drifting away when I stepped on the path.

OBEY HALFWAY?

Yes, my God, I will obey,
(If I can fit it in today,
And if it doesn't take too long,
And if it's not the same old song.)

Test me, Master, so I can show,
That I'm as pure as driven snow!
I promise I'll not let you down,
(Unless another gets the crown.)

Yes, my Lord, I'm an eager mate,
(But just don't make me have to wait.
Don't let me worry or test my nerve.
Make my pathway straight, so I can't swerve.)

Let's plow ahead, God, just you and me,
(But only as far as I can see,
And let's only tackle some simple tasks,
So, I can wear my "happy" mask.)

There's nothing, Master, that we can't do!

(I'll have some coffee; you pull us through.
I don't like long days, the heat, or crowds,
And whisper, please, don't shout out loud.)

Yes, my Lord, I will obey!
I'll do anything on any day!
Me? Reservations? Why do you ask?
You only have to name the task!

NEVER ENOUGH

God, you haven't blessed me, not nearly enough,
My life's been hard, my way's too tough.
My caviar is not the best!
My Lamborghini burns Hi-Test!
I need more rooms to fill with stuff!

C'mon, God, you want the best for me?
If I'm still toiling, how can that be?
I can only play golf twice a week,
I can't afford Aspen at its peak,
You aren't pulling your weight, God, can't you see?

I'm supposed to win, so others drool,
Filthy rich and, oh, so cool!
I'm your ambassador, so hold me up,
Makes others covet my trophy cup!
A pedestal, please, not a small step stool!

And, notoriety! Hey, what do you say about that?
My wallet's too thin, my waist, too fat!
There are still a few who don't know my name,

That's right, God, I need much more fame!
No champion wins with a step that's flat.

I bought in on glitter, on glam and glitz,
A penthouse suite atop the Ritz,
You're just not holding up your end,
The other guy's got a contract, penned!
And he's been in my ear and giving me fits!

I want it all, and I want it now,
Crikey, Lord, holy cow,
Bless me more—and more—and more,
Make my every shot a half-court score!
Then... everyone will ask me, "How?"

I AM THE G.O.A.T.

I deserve it for I'm entitled,
Exceptional, free, unfettered, unbridled.
No pesky restraints bind my thoughts or my deeds,
I can wander and drift where my wild fancy leads!

No law can control me or what I can do.
I focus on me; I'm not focused on you.
This big world serves me and has only one function,
And that's to keep me away from a tough moral junction.

For if I'm not chided, confronted or called,
Upon some good Master's carpet for venting my gall,
Or made to face or examine my wrong, wayward ways,
I'm content to just waste and to wane all my days.

My friends—all enablers—serve me ever so well.
They polish and spit shine and dress up my hell,
They normalize all of my abnormal acts,
They make lies seem like truths, when they're spinning the
facts.

"Each for himself," their sweet mantra goes,
"You're an island, young man! You're the G.O.A.T! You're a
pro!"
"Don't cast them a glance. Don't look into the eyes,
Of those who'd take you away from your temporal prize!"

For in the end, I feel certain, when the footlights go out,
The final tally of swag was what life was about!
It's what I had in my bank; it's the stuff I amassed,
Living life to the fullest and just having a blast!

Yet, a small part of me wonders when the yes-men all leave,
When there's no one but me left that I must deceive,
When my crowd finds a new face that they'd rather follow,
When my senses and self both grow dark, bland and hollow,

When the fog that's invaded just refuses to lift,
When the scales now won't balance and the sifter won't sift,
Before that voice's soft whisper falls silent, quits trying,
Will I finally listen or resign then to dying.

UNSEEN, BUT NOT UNKNOWN

In that place where matter does not even matter,
Where atoms and ions are neither leaner nor fatter,
(They're not part of discussion for they do not exist),
There are only intangibles that make up the list.

Not subject to measure, not subject to proof,
It's used to ridicule, slander and spoof.
This dimension, this space, this world, this penumbra,
Has no deltas, no symbols, no theorems, no numbers.

It's a cosmos of notions, of ideas and thoughts,
Of concepts, of feelings—elusive, uncaught,
Where the powers that govern betwixt and between,
Divide into camps of what good and what's mean.

Not a speck or a jot of dust passes there,
Not a breath can be taken, for no rarified air,
Supports any creature or sustains carbon life,
Yet, forces do battle over goodness and strife.

No, atoms? No matter. But it matters a lot,

For the now and hereafter, whether pleasant or not,
Are played out inside it, there is so much at stake,
It's where hard truth is tested, and eternity waits.

Can you see it and sense it; does it make you just squirm,
This place in the nether, with "new" substance—just terms—
With descriptions in lieu of a sight, sound or feel,
But with a presence not just as, but, frankly, more real?

There are alphabet letters that float in the soup,
They combine by design and then exit the loop,
Colliding, repelling, forming sinew and derma,
As if forming a world, but without terra firma.

The building blocks there? The real DNA?
Of the strings and the strands of the new night and day,
Are the groans and the sighs that compose terms and words,
That mortal man sometimes, by chance, may have heard.

Where do those names come from; where are those words
born?
They don't fall from a truck on a bleak, frosty morn.
They don't burst from a shell or ignite from thin air,
They come from that place that's not here and not there.

Words have no dimensions, but they carry such weight!
No sense can perceive them, though their gravity, great.
No thing in this world can explain, don't you see,
How such words can take hold; how such words come to be.

Yet, a man catches glimpses, in groups or alone,
Of words that define just whose side he is on.
Does he move to the light or shrink, fade to the dark,
The dichotomy, truly, is clear and it's stark.

14

Each word has an opposite, it is what it's not,
Peace? Absence of strife. Cold? Absence of hot.
There's a distance, a gulf, between these conventions,
But they manifest order and Holy intentions.

We've kenned some of the language in the past and until,
We know the divine and see over the hill.
Integrity, evil, righteousness and, yes, sin,
Aren't of earth, moon or sky, and they never have been.

In the grand scheme of things, from poor man's point of view,
The words float in the ether, the primordial stew.
The Neologist, the Great One, holds them firmly, I've heard,
From the very beginning, He has been "the Word."

DO GOOD

I waded in, I tip-toed lightly,
I dragged myself (wrongly? rightly?)
I questioned, argued, thought I'd bail,
Kicking, screaming, dug in my nails.

I cashed in friends, for what, I thought.
My psyche bloodied, I jousted, fought,
I twisted, turned, was blown by winds,
Got caught in webs the spider spins.

Convinced myself that bad was good,
That flowers bloom in a concrete 'hood,
That a loving God would never let
The misguided lose their souls, why fret?

That a narrow path was not the way,
That smooth, broad road seems great, I'd say,
And that tiny path was hard, I'd mention,
While the other was paved with good intention.

For too long I straddled the space between.

Just numb, I guess, not nice, not mean,
Not hot, not cold, just shrouded sight,
A deer caught between two beams of light.

Each light illumined, I could not choose,
One seemed a winner; I thought I'd lose.
If I took the path with few upon it,
Would I regret it? Would I have blown it?

"Move!" I shouted to no one there,
"Do something!" I screamed, I didn't care,
Then, "Save me!" I cried… Where'd that come from?
A message stored when I was young?

Could I really expect a helping hand?
To heal, direct this broken man,
To light my way, to guide me home,
To leave sad loneliness alone?

"On my schedule, God, not yours, but mine!
If you don't care, then I'll be fine."
I'm sure that final strand was frayed.
I resolved to sleep in the bed I made.

Then—one day—I saw the curtain lift,
I don't know why, I just took the gift.
My mental sky became clear blue,
I learned a truth I never knew.

It was never truly about just me!
But also, others lost on the same, sad sea.
If I could find a peace through Him,
My purpose was to share with them.

No longer would I search in vain,
To swallow gnats for shallow gain,
For with faith but like a grain of salt,
I let go companions, sin and fault.

What once were halting, tiny steps,
Are now great strides with life and pep.
Where once I faltered, with fearful spasms,
Now I boldly leap the broadest chasms.

Who could know that meaning in this short life,
Is not to outrun trials and strife,
But to live for others, as we feel we should,
Do good, do good, do good, do good.

ALL THE MONEY

All the money in the world,
A handsome man, the pretty girl,
The car that turns the haughty head,
Status, power, you can all drop dead!

A life of ease, you don't know pain,
Just sunny skies, no chance of rain.
A road that's level, no dips ahead,
Will make you jump straight out of bed!

You have this world right by its tail,
Though dog-eat-dog, you cannot fail,
Or... so you think, for a day will come,
When fame and fortune call you a bum.

Maybe that happens overnight,
The market crashes, your crowd takes flight,
That car you've driven so hard and fast,
Finds a post or rail, with pain that lasts.

Or, maybe you'll have a gentle ride,

On a slow, receding, ebbing tide.
You'll barely notice the rising temp,
Because you thought you were exempt.

Will you still revel when that day arrives?
The self-made man with type-A drive,
Who thought he needed just himself,
Putting everything else upon a shelf.

You planned for all, except for this,
You blew it off, without a kiss.
Who would you be stripped down to dust?
A naked soul, no God to trust?

It's not too late, friend, see the light!
What you think you have, your status, might,
Mean nothing in the scheme of things,
When you're carried on angels' or demons' wings.

Make friends with Jesus, his saints, and those,
You've overlooked or looked down your nose.
Hear His voice, obey His word,
You've no excuse, for NOW, you've heard.

WHERE HAS MY HOLY SPIRIT GONE?

Where has my Holy Spirit gone,
I asked myself, when all alone.
My joy had left me, my hopes were dashed.
Would ending it really be so rash?

Too long I had refused to hear,
That it was others I should hold so dear,
And not myself, not only me,
My friends moved on and set me free.

To drift, to float on currents cold,
To dance on streets of foolish gold,
For fleeting moments with a happy glimmer,
While my Spirit stewed and my eyes grew dimmer.

That siren song that the whole world sings
Just got too loud, and that's the thing,
It drowned out the voice I once had heard,
That helped me find peace and to live the Word.

So, here I sit, it is dark, I hurt,
My life is shallow, my patience, curt,
I love no one, not even me,
And from myself I cannot flee.

My flesh controls my every act,
Even when I know I'm bad, in fact.
I justify telling God He's wrong,
Then pay the price I saw all along.

If only I could hear that voice,
I might find strength to make the choice,
Of serving others—and not myself—
And to put the old me on a shelf.

If I were gentle, if I were kind,
Maybe others would see and come and find,
A wretch with value and lift me up,
And place to my lips, a loving cup.

Where are you, Spirit? Why can't I hear,
The guidance once whispered in my ear?
Where have you gone? Please return to me,
This time, I'll heed and bend my knee.

And then, so faintly, like far away,
Like in the distance, I heard Him say,
"I was waiting for you to come home, my son,
You just needed faith in me, the One."

We have been here, and watching, we've been leaning on
fences,
Just waiting for you to come to your senses,
That all of these things you know you need
Are free to you, son, with the faith of a seed.

"So, come home to us now, hold others up high,
Serve your brothers and sisters and you'll live and not die!
Ask me for guidance," the Spirit then said,
And the sunrise that morning warmed a soul without dread.

LIFE IS RUNNING

Life is running—grab it—quick
Apply some glue, make it stick
Seize that smile we saw between
The tick of twenty and old nineteen.

Hold that memory of glory, gold,
Of conquest, soaring, of being bold,
A crash is coming, just like the waves,
You'll be dropped, replaced by current faves.

You're a ticket, number, a photo op
To be forgotten with a jump, skip, hop,
Once you're drained and pained, your value gone,
It's next man up, you'll head for home.

But where is home, you poor, poor wretch,
Now even Fido won't play catch,
You'll be alone—forever—think that through
Worse that anyone ever knew.

I was once like you, but I stepped off,

Turned in my card, accepted scoff.
With eyes turned upward, my soul found peace,
No longer chasing a golden fleece.

You had a chance, remember when?
You had an offer, a gift, but then,
You thought yourself your only Master,
If you could only run a little faster.

LIKE JAMES

Even His family thought Him mad,
Despite the miracles and victories had,
When even demons obeyed His word,
Who am I to doubt the news I've heard?

He told me of the unseen world,
Let me glimpse the future time unfurled.
He spoke the book to ancient ones,
For all to follow, for all His sons.

So, if you think me silly, please,
When I close my eyes and am on my knees,
I ask my God to lead the way,
I'm happy that I made your day.

NONE SO BLIND

There was a time I heard you clearly,
So, fully, deeply, not just merely,
When my walls collapse, when arrows fly,
When storm clouds choke my sunny sky.

Your voice ebbed, as my hearing faded,
My storehouse lost and always raided,
No will to fight when the cuts add up,
No strength left when I've drained my cup.

There was a time that we spoke often,
My edges hard, you helped me soften.
Enemies knew us, called off attacks,
You know, I don't think I really lacked

Anything. What's up? Are we still tight?
Can I squeeze you in when time is right?
My days are crowded, maybe next week?
Chaotic, hectic. Hmmm, looking bleak.

If I can only find a minute,

If I can only manage, then it,
Will get better, we'll turn things around,
I'll hear you again, turn up the sound.

Get back in step, renew our climb,
If I talk to you and share some time.
Yes! That's the plan! I will call next week,
Too busy right now, I've got a leak.

THE SCALES

When in sleep I died, the U-Haul truck,
Stayed in park, I was out of luck.
My collected things? All left behind.
My baggage? Just my soul and mind.

My soul was all that made me, me,
A battered personality,
So perfect before the world took hold,
And stuffed it—tattered—in a wicked mold.

My mind? The sum of all I did,
And thought and said and showed and hid.
Those countless memories that formed each day,
Were never lost, just tucked away.

Before I reached the pearly gates,
A rest stop, where a scale awaits,
My Earthly weight on one pan sits,
My shiny things—wow—check out the glitz!

On the other pan, I climbed, forlorn,

My soul was weighty when I was born,
But that worn out tire, a nail invaded,
And now it seemed flat, I sat and waited.

My mind, I thought might tip the scale,
I've thought of numbers, words and whales,
Of clouds, of weather, of things that bite,
But they came to naught, they were just too light.

If only I had thought of neighbors,
And shared life's moments, happy, savored,
My mind would weight ten thousand pounds!
My pan would plummet to the ground!

Resigned, I shivered, defeated, cold,
I pulled a level, some great gears rolled.
The pans were moving, I cried, "I'm lost!"
Life weight? Too heavy! My soul, the cost.

With downcast eyes, the scales, mid-air,
Some added weight? What was it there?
The hand of God? A finger placed,
Upon the scale to give me grace!

For way, way back, I don't know when,
I met the Lord and asked Him then,
If I should die before I'd wake,
That my poor soul, He'd be sure to take.

WE'RE ALL SINNERS

We're all sinners, everyone,
Our nature, history, cry out loud.
Stained glass colors of filtered sun,
Light upon us as hope or shroud.

For in this hall a mystery brews,
A battle wages for living, dead,
While moist eyes close, on hallowed pews,
The Spirit hovers overhead.

So, bring more sin into this place!
Watch the heavenly force assemble!
God's power, goodness, surpassing grace,
Make evil ones flee and tremble!

If we are sure that God abides,
That our faith is strong and right,
Eternal light we dare not hide,
Leave God to show His might!

Invite the lost from near and far,
Throw open doors and wash their feet,
Let the Spirit convict them as they are,
To walk His path and not the street.

GIVE CHRIST YOUR KEYS

When you think that you've hit bottom,
But you find it's deeper still,
When the gotchas and the got-ems,
Have broken bones and heart and will,
When the ones you love have failed you,
When they've fled the sight of blood,
And you're all alone, and you've said adieu,
Awaiting splat and thud,
When the worst thing that can ever hap,
Is now cresting o'er the rise,
When you've sat upon the Devil's lap,
And you're caught up in his lies,
When the end's not near—it's come and gone—
When there's nowhere left to turn,
Remember Jesus can drive you home.
Give Him the keys and learn.
For you cannot fall too far for Him,
No problem, that abyss,
He's a cushion, a net, a chute, a shim,
Forgiving failure, fault and miss.

So, fear not, free faller, enjoy the ride.
When the world nips at your neck,
Show your face, no need to hide.
He offers grace, and will save your hide,
Don't drive yourself, and wreck.

MY CHOICE

My spirit straddles air and earth,
Yours, too, you know, from your day of birth,
Like one foot planted on firm, dry land,
While the other one sinks in loose, wet sand.

Required to choose, with poor instruction,
Destined to shine or face destruction,
Forced to peel away some opaque gauze,
To find the purpose, to see the cause.

No wonder those on the broad, smooth path,
Can't see the coming judgment wrath,
Seduced by glowing feeds on screens,
Tumbling, sliding in a crash careen.

Cataract lenses that hide the light,
That keeps the soul from taking flight.
It takes clearest vision and a mighty leap,
To see awake what dwells in sleep.

Still deep down, way, way down deep,

All sense the Reaper, though not all weep.
A light within, a warmth, a glow,
There's the Truth that many more should know.

Death's not the end; it's just the start,
Of a living or of a dying heart,
So we must choose which step to take,
Into the sky or the fiery lake.

My spirit straddles air and earth,
My choice foreshadows grief or mirth,
For where I plant my weight these days,
Leads to His gift or the price I'll pay.

YOU ARE FAULTY

You are faulty, I know you're blemished,
And so am I, but God's not finished.
This simple truth that God has shone,
Makes me drop the judgment stone.

Do we falter? Of course, we do!
Anxious for the other shoe
To drop without God's watchful hand,
We misplace trust in fallen man.

Controlling little, deciding much,
Without the Master's guiding touch,
We're dangling headfirst, the deep abyss,
Awaits us, if His truth we miss.

Our God is good! His love abounds,
He revels in the lost sheep found!
Give in to faith, abide, obey,
And seek to follow Him each day.

And like the monkeys on the shelf,
See no evil, save in yourself,
Speak no evil, it serves no good,
And hear not the evil that Satan would.

WHY GATHER?

Why should we gather; why should we meet?
A curt "Hello" is not enough, when passing on the street.
We need to know the ones we trust, the ones who know our
Lord,
And the ones to keep with watchful eye, the ones who lead
the horde.

You need to know the inner me, I need to know your heart,
That's quite a task, when walking fast, and moving far apart.
But in warm environs of a home with welcome table set,
We can probe and seek, our minds at work, to stave off deep
regret.

Or, 'neath a tree, beside a brook, or on some hallowed
ground,
I can find the "you" that's kept inside, you might sense
without a sound.
When two or more are gathered, and when pure hearts are on
display,
The hazy smoke of pretense clears, true discourse leads
the way.

And, if that discourse, and if those hearts, see far beyond today,
Toward restful homes for faithful souls, then the Spirit will find a way.
For the one who's further down the path, whose steps are near the gate,
To lead, encourage, influence, pray, to tarry—it's worth the wait.

THE KEEPER OF THE LIGHT

Sometimes the mist and fog would call, so black and thick,
like a widow's shawl,
And horns and bells, oft anchored deep, pierced not the veil
that came with sleep.
Great storms were normal on that old coast, for nature threw
much, so she could boast,
Of pelting rain and of wind so fierce, one could not tell what's
far or near us.

But no matter what, he rose from bed, trudging the path that
others dread,
Climbed the steps, faced dark and wind, and lit the beacon
once again.
He cast the light far out to sea and said a prayer for you
and me,
So, ships and boats upon the blue would miss the perils the
keeper knew.

Week by week, and year by year, he persevered, with faithful
cheer,

Kept the candle shining through a polished lens, guiding
grateful sailors to their travels' ends.
You were the keeper, and we will miss, your gentle grace,
remember this,
God put you there to mind the flame, until that day His new
keeper came.

THE CALENDAR

The calendar has turned yet once again,
Another year with your best friend,
Each year is different from the rest,
Each year you're being greatly blessed.

Your life is strong, on solid ground,
Cemented with the love you've found,
Keep joy and life within you hearts,
Together and when you're far apart.

Take this blessing from far away,
To keep you steady day-by-day,
And know that you are in the prayers,
Of many, those who truly care.

WHEN SHADOWS FALL

I ponder much when shadows fall,
My life, my death, a curtain call.
The ones before, those yet to be,
The torch my father handed me.

He left, no words, no time, no voice,
God called him home; he had no choice.
I carried on, it's what I do,
One day I'll pass the torch to you.

Advice? I don't remember much.
Affection? Maybe just a touch.
But somehow, I picked up what I should,
Be strong, be brave, fight hard, do good.

We are pilgrims, you and I,
Born of dust, blown upward, high,
Straddling lives in separate realms,
Who should we trust behind the helm?

I've sailed so long through cloud and mist,
Unsure of most, but sure in this,
The Master of my ship of fate,
Will dock us at the Pearly Gate.

SO WHAT NOW, MY LORD?

I sat in the shadows for so many years,
With nothing expected and nothing required,
Content to observe, with no need to shed tears,
A hollow apprentice, tell me why was I hired?

I watched and I waited, my mind half asleep,
As my master took over, putting troubles to bed.
I saw him exhausted, saw him sad, saw him weep,
Saw him grieve o'er his charges, with eyes sunken and red.

Yet, he toiled for his Master, never once to complain,
His recompense small from what I could see,
His progress was slow, if at all, in his pain,
And only so often would he glance down at me.

His stare, when he glanced, was a deep, piercing gaze,
Was he trying to welcome, was he warning, a scare?
That the task would consume him for the rest of his days,
I thought not of the future, could I even dare?

Then one day my master awoke not from slumber,

His closed eyes now still, he entered his rest,
Others looked up at me, they were calling my number,
I retreated, defeated, was I up to the test?

But I heard a small voice, once I shut out the noise,
"Take courage, my son, I will stand by your side.
I will lead all the way, you, the weakest of boys,
No one can oppose you, with you'll abide."

REMEMBER (TO LOVE)

If I don't dress the way you do,
If I slip on a worn-out shoe,
If words or phrases I don't know,
If I can't drop a nice "bon mot",
If my meal's not fit for king or queen,
Maybe just a bun or a can of beans,
If my hands are worn, my nails, a mess,
If I look like I have lived duress,
If I don't bow or kneel on time,
If I can't hear the sacred chime,
If my memory fails with the age-old creed,
Some ancient bishop penned to lead,
The babes in faith to fall in place
With this or that group's path to grace,
Just know that I'm a child, like you,
My Father loves us both, we two,
Though He placed us here on different paths,
Toward joyful hope, away from wrath.
So, if I love you, and you love me,
And we both love Him, He'll set us free,

From the bonds and chains of mortal men,
And though we differ, we will be friends.

WHAT WAS SIN THINKING?

What was sin thinking on the way to the cross?
That black stain on hearts, that pain and that loss,
From a humble beginning in a garden back when,
To that lying in wait over there, round the bend.

Sin woke up that morning, with a stretch and a yawn,
Feeling pretty darn good on that Good Friday morn.
Sin's daily agenda, its schedule, for sure,
Was misery-spreading, thinking there was no cure.

Principalities, powers, rulers of night,
Invisible kings, and those haters of light,
The Devil, his demons and who knows what more,
Spent that morning at leisure, 'fore that knock at the door.

We think singular "sin" to encompass a horde,
Of those words, thoughts and deeds that oppose our just
Lord.
And those bits that infect us, like hate and like doubt,
Are the army that Jesus would take on and would rout.

That great mass of evil, quintillions of bits,
Some ancient, some present, some still in the pit.
It's a thing, it was there, on that hill, on that day,
I wonder what happened, did it fight, what'd it say?

Did it know that the power of the dark side was done?
Did it know that the man on the cross was the one?
Who would snuff them all out, crush them all with His will,
On that barren and rocky and sorrowful hill?

I imagine, like ants, sin ascended that mound,
The legends, reluctant, called forth by a sound,
Beyond human hearing, no mere trumpet of man,
A triumphant blast for God's well-thought-out plan.

That call to that cohort to gather, amass,
Could not be resisted, it came full and fast,
Like the animal pairs in the great Ark of old,
It climbed up the cross and the Master took hold.

Each one had a name, each one had a place,
Each one an appendage to a poor, human face,
Each one had a stronghold in somebody's life,
Each one had a mission of death and of strife.

A great unseen battle took place there, I know,
Jesus fought the battalions brought forth by His foe.
When not one remained and there were none to replenish,
Only then He went home, satisfied it was finished.

I think sin's a coward, it would run from that task,
If its legs were not chained to that man on the mast.
For surely sin knew it was meeting its end,
When the Lord was in sight, now, just as back then.

So, what did sin say to Jesus that eve,
When He took them all on, so that not one could leave?
"We surrender!" for starters, all the demons would cry,
To the Ruler of earth and the Ruler of sky.

Yes, the darkness bowed—trembling—and fear gripped
them all,
With His breath they were vanquished. They were bugs on a
wall.
Wave after wave, they vanished, were gone,
Before He would sit on His heavenly throne.

Christ fought them for hours to clean up our mess,
He took on our sin—that we must confess—
And when the day ended and when the smoke cleared,
Our sins were wiped clean, and the angels all cheered!

So, what was sin thinking that day at the cross?
It was learning the lesson of just who's the boss!
It's weak, futile efforts to maintain control,
Christ crushed and defeated to salvage your soul.

HE WAS WITH ME ALL THE TIME

He always had my back, because He always knew my heart,
Even when sin was in control, He played a vital part.
He begged, He reasoned, He challenged and pled,
To my hollow soul, to my empty heart and to my spirit almost dead.

He was always present, always near, always earnest, patient, clear,
I had no answers to the questions posed by the whispering voice beside my ear.
"Why are you here? Where will you go, when the TV screen turns into snow?
Are your days upright or all for naught? Must life be futile and sorrow-fraught?"

"What do you know about Truth and love?
Is there something more? A God above?
How did this planet come to be?
Can you live a joyous life? Be free?"

Serious queries, gentle nudges, for a mind that ached, inquiring,

Always leading, never pushing, though time was short, expiring,

Giving me, and my free will, the chance to think things through,

To choose my course, to make my bed, but I think He always knew.

Each question, too deep, but I came to feel there was no more need to roam,

I concluded I was too wonderfully made for earth to be my home.

So, finally, I yielded, turned my life around, and He stepped inside on holy ground,

The bad guys fled, sweet peace took hold, my spirit lives, my purpose found!

FEAR

Fear is evil, a lie, a word,
That Satan uses to drive the herd,
That makes us question, makes us doubt,
The truth we know, within, without.

We find fear in the shadow-places,
In unkind speech, on scornful faces,
In deep, dark holes, where joy retreats,
In moments that linger 'tween hurt-heart beats.

We find fear when we try to see,
Beyond the now, across that sea,
Where the other side is not in sight,
Though we know the map is sure and right.

Fear sails within an unseen realm,
A ship, a liar at the helm.
And "lifelines" that it tosses out,
Are just cords to strangle, deadly doubt.

So, what's a mortal man to do,

When hope seems old and fear seems new?
When the gulf is wide, when little's left,
When the heart and mind seem frayed and cleft?

Well, fear can't abide where faith resides,
It slithers and runs and ducks and hides.
We have the light, we have the door,
To banish fear forevermore!

Consult the manual, the Book, God's own,
A hundred times, you're not alone.
Why would you fear what Satan throws,
When God stands strong, deflecting blows?

You are a child of heaven now!
Just lean into your yoke, and plow,
The burden's light, the harvest sure,
A drop of faith is still the cure.

You know that God is in control,
He won't desert one precious soul,
He will not leave you, He leads the way,
So, you won't fall as evil's prey.

PATIENCE

There's a moment just waiting, when your life is a rush,
When the pot will not boil, when your tax is late,
When the kids won't get dressed or you still need your blush.
That moment is patience. Will you put down your weight?

When you're in a tight race to rise up on some list,
With not enough minutes to get the job done
And you're running so late there's no time for a kiss,
Patience slows down the pace. Will you stroll and not run?

Satan wants you to think that your days are so numbered
That you'll miss something important, if you don't speed
about,
But in truth, when you're running, it's like you have
slumbered
And the scenery blurs, when you're going all out.

Can you find the time to let life come to you?
Don't overlap living, you can't get it all in,
Without slowing your pace, what you'll have missed when
you're through

Are those tender, sweet seconds of what could have been.

Just look first to Jesus for the Spirit is there
To help you go slowly, to give grace and forgive.
Inhale deeply, smile warmly, give another your chair
As patience settles into the home where you live.

PERSERVERANCE

The world is graying, the shadows fall,
Our faith is challenged at every turn.
What once was clear to one and all,
The foolish seek to thwart and burn.

Thank you. God, for wisdom day and night,
For lessons taught and guidance shown
That help me know my path is right,
To lead me to my place at home.

Without your strength, I would not find mine,
I could not bear my enemy's wrath,
But You comfort me with a peace divine,
Bought with blood, you mark my path.

Beyond the horizon, I clearly see
Above the noisy crowd, I clearly hear,
So, I push onward to draw closer to Thee
Enjoying the journey, willing to share.

LONGSUFFERING

Father, forgive them, for they know not
They lack the wisdom to discern.
They vacillate, blowing both cold and hot
It pains me they just will not learn.

When one grows tired, another takes his place,
A legion queues up against me,
We stand toe-to-toe and face-to-face,
My patience ebbs, my strength wants to flee.

Father, I know my mission, I know my post,
To hold the line, to show no fear.
And with the Helper, the Holy Ghost,
Tomorrow, I will still be here.

My task is not to win the fight,
My role is not to slay the beast,
My task is but to last the night,
To show them that they may not feast.

For when morning comes, I'll rise again.
They may question my sanity, but not my resolve,
My patience, though frayed and worn pencil-thin,
Let them marvel at how I evolve!

AT JESUS' FEET

I imagine sitting at Jesus' feet,
Or walking with Him on a dusty street,
Or sharing a meal round a crackling fire,
Or learning the truth and setting sights higher.

I imagine the crowds, the happy, the healed,
The words of salvation, the future revealed,
The gift of His grace, His forgiveness of sin,
I imagine the mess that my life could have been.

But I shut out the other, the cost and the cross,
I run from the pain and the hurt and the loss,
That my witness will bring me, as sure as the dawn,
If I stand up for Him, once He has gone.

I welcome the sun, I curse when there's rain,
I revel in warmth, in the cold I feel pain.
How I yearn the world's touch, for the pat on my back,
By those who don't love me, they despise me, in fact.

I am a wretch, I am worthy of naught,

I'm the flickering flame of the candle I bought.
My resolve ebbs and flows like the tides of my life,
I'm a coward, who cowers when confronted with strife.

"Remember Lot's wife!" I remember her well,
She turned and looked back, she was under the spell,
Her eyes were not fixed on her future, her prize,
She was suck in the valley, she saw not over the rise.

I need a grip, not a vision or sign,
I know what I need to walk tall down the line.
I need just to have strength in the shadow of death,
To hold fast to my Master, and He'll do the rest.

HEAVEN'S GATE

A small bateau put out to sea,
With Jesus at the helm, and me,
A fishing vessel, small, but true,
We hope to land a precious few.

We had success, that spawned great hope,
More boats were needed, more nets, more rope.
A fleet, the Master sought to build,
To muster many, our ranks to fill.

And so it was, down through the ages,
Our numbers grew in spurts and stages,
But even then, our tiny craft.
Matched not some waves that chased us aft.

For while the truth remained the same,
Salvation in the Master's name,
The evil one was always near,
To swamp our boats, to curry fear.

And some—a few—succumbed to that,

Forgot the Truth, threw in the hat,
The message, wet, got watered down,
Because some on board liked not its sound.

So, over time, some small boats drifted,
Forgetting words the Master gifted,
'Til a precious few remained in Truth,
Tied to the mast of the crusade's youth.

Tactics changed, we came together,
And built a ship to withstand the weather,
And we all set sail again that day,
Knowing we'd best what came our way.

The message was our treasure chest,
We fought off pirates, Satan's best.
Our course secure and true and straight,
We sailed on to dock at Heaven's gate.

But on the way, we pulled you from,
A leaky, messy, drifting drum,
And all aboard, through tempest's gale,
Knew you were why He had us sail.

THE BUS FROM BROAD STREET

It's a bald-faced lie we can tell ourselves,
None left behind, none on the shelf.
For if all of the dogs get to go on to heaven,
Then certainly Mary Beth, Roger and Kevin,

Will join us there, though they have no use,
For Jesus' love; they just hurl abuse,
Toward those who accept and who dwell in the Truth—
The Gospel—ubiquitous, from everyone's youth.

They think it's so cool to cast put-down aspersions,
(Satan's stories, we know, come in so many versions).
Knowing not what they say, well, it's sad and it's tough,
Will Christ's plea to the Father be nearly enough?

Will His bad moon warnings, specific and plain,
Fade as lost souls are flushed down a dark, swirly drain?
Must we acknowledge Christ now or can we just wait,
For a strong write-in vote at the old, Pearly Gate?

That line would be long—the damned seeking rest—

When the Broad bus dumps souls at St. Peter's desk,
But nowhere is it written in that Great Book of Life,
That admission is granted for lovers of strife.

An afterlife pardon? A do-over? Reprieve?
An "I didn't mean what I said, so you don't have to leave!"
An "I was just kidding!" Why would you expect it?
It's all in the Book, but you didn't respect it...

Does "only" mean "only"? Does "the" suggest "many"?
Is belief in a lie, if sincere, good as any?
Would the Alpha/Omega give shifting directions?
Or give changeless instructions that don't need corrections?

Do you truly know Jesus, or will you just roll the dice?
Does God have a new app changing naughty to nice?
Will the Word sync with the lost, or exact the last toll?
Will the snake's eyes lay claim to your eternal soul?

HOW DO THEY KNOW?

How do they know that I belong,
To Jesus Christ, my Master,
Or that I choose the narrow pathway home,
To veer far from sure disaster?

They know because I freely aid,
The travelers that I meet,
A crust of bread, some Gatorade,
Some shade to beat the heat.

A helping hand on a rocky road,
No judgments do I make,
An extra shoulder to ease the load,
A soul may be at stake!

They know I'm His without a word,
Because of how I live.
They know because they know I heard
Him tell His sheep to give.

GOD'S LAW

I do not fear God's righteous laws,
I don't slow down, I do not pause,
I don't retreat, I don't lose grit,
Because I lack a perfect fit.

I love His standard; I know I'll fail,
But I have the key to escape from jail.
That key? It's Jesus! He keeps me free,
While others sink in a restless sea.

God's law is perfect, absolute,
I'm mortal and with ill repute,
But I can look and in awe stare,
At the target God has placed up there.

I dare not change a single word,
Nor excuse parts to please the herd,
Who want to sin, reminded not,
What's watered down can make them hot.

His law is like a bright, white light,

That shreds the darkness, splits the night,
A beacon that will draw me near,
So, my rowboat docks at a sturdy pier.

But mostly, His law just let's me know,
That He is God, not me, and so,
I just submit in humbled state,
And revel—for my God is great!

STORM CLOUDS

I met a man with a hardened heart,
Who had the world, or at least a part,
He surfed the wave of wealth and praise,
Hanged ten in sunshine all his days.

Until one day, the sun withdrew,
And storm clouds came, a normal new,
And all his power, and all his fame,
Failed, so he set to assign the blame.

His friends, he thought, could it be they,
Who left him high and dry one day?
And how about those in business deals?
The ones with whom He'd lie and steal.

The government, he thought, that was in his pocket,
Abandoned him, like a booster rocket.
He resigned to pull within his shell,
A cooped-up and darkened, living hell.

Our paths crossed one day on a busy street,

His voice was hollow, his eyes were weak,
I sensed he needed a prayerful word,
Just from the little I saw and heard.

"May I pray for you?" I whispered, squeaked,
"Don't bother," he said, no interest piqued.
From the awkward pause that then ensued,
The grace of God just gushed and oozed.

"It's not a bother," I finally said,
"You are my brother, and you need bread,
The bread of life, you need to know it.
God sent me here today to show it."

"I'm going to pray for you today,
And even if you walk away,
My prayer will be that your heart softens,
And God's blessings find you now, and often."

And then we parted, that's all I know,
A handful of words were the seeds I'd sow.
Did fruit spring forth? It's in God's hands,
He holds the glass and the hour's sands.

NO COMPROMISE

There is no compromise with Christ,
Salvation has been fairly priced.
The rich, young ruler walked away,
No bargaining what he'd have to pay.

There is no compromise with God,
The pathway home—an uphill trod.
He sees the pitfalls up ahead,
If we turn away, our souls are dead.

The Holy Spirit requires we hear,
To learn and live, to draw us near.
Vain debate is not a useful art,
To align with God a wayward heart.

The contract, deal, agreement, pact,
Is simple, clear, straightforward, fact.
To enter through the Pearly Gate,
Surrender all. Our God is great!

PRAYER

"Must I pray out loud?" signed a poor muted man.
"Or intertwine fingers?" asked a man with no hand.
"Or close my two eyes?" one blind man asked.
"And kneeling," asked one, "if in bed I am fast?"

"Hey! Fancy words?" joked a man from down south,
"They're too big to fit into my mind or my mouth!"
"What does God expect?", I voiced about prayer,
"Clean, combed and scrubbed? Must a suit be my wear?"

If I need not speak sounds or clasp both of my hands,
Eyes open, eyes shut; I can kneel, I can stand,
No repeating of words that some ancient had penned,
While ensconced in a tower or other place he was in.

No need to bow (if my neck will not move),
Just what is the act that my God WILL approve?
Well, God knows my mind, my thoughts, and my heart,
My sins, my failures, my faith, all my parts.

He knows that I still strain to hear His soft voice,

That I seek His will daily with each, single choice.
He knows that I know that my sins are so great,
And that even when finished, I'll have much left on my plate.

He just wants to know me; he wants good, honest talk,
He wants to join with me on a slow, ambling walk.
As my life's desperation dissolves, dissipates,
While we meander together, and time pauses, awaits.

I treasure those moments, in each hectic day,
When we talk and He tells me, "Calm down, you're okay."
And even if I have not said the right word,
From the peace that I gain, I am sure that He heard.

BE CAREFUL WHO HAS YOUR EAR

"Disobey, break the law, reject, ignore, rebel!
Do what you like, take what you want, just do it, what the
hell?
The needy? Well, they're just losers. They aren't like you," he
said.
"They've gotten just what they deserve; they might as well be
dead."

I was so special—one of a kind—my wrongs could not be
wrong!
I was followed like a rock star, I had stage and screen and
song!
I didn't even pay for that! He gave it to me for free!
He said that I had liberty, so make it all about me!

What a nice guy, or so I thought, it sounded all so good,
Live it up, let it all hang out, live my way just like I should,
But now, it's dark and silent—and hot; I've hit a wall,
And wouldn't you know that dirty rat will not accept my call?

THE QUESTION

How can I know if my soul is safe?
A child of God or a poor, lost waif?
Will I join the banquet at the wedding feast,
Or be ON the menu of the devil, the beast?

I chanted the words, I've stood, and I've sat,
And I've kneeled and bowed down; I've done all of that.
I don't know much, but I am certain of this,
Just calling Christ, Lord, will not guarantee bliss.

Let me think for a moment; let me think this thing through,
Faith and belief, say some verses, are enough and will do.
I think that I have those, but I still have some doubts,
What's missing? Uneasy! Got to figure this out!

Have I truly MET Christ? Have I heard his clear voice?
Has my whole life changed? Do I make the right choice?
Does the Holy Spirit relax and recline in me,
When I'm eating some popcorn or watching TV?

Do I shed a real tear if a Christian should stumble?

Do I shout The Good News or do I "hem-haw" and mumble?
Have I passed that innate and strong yearning to shine,
To be the one at the center, not once, but each time?

Am I willing to give and to help and to share,
To empty my storehouse to God—in His care,
Do I seek to serve others in their times of need,
To the point that it hurts; to the point that I'll bleed?

And do I call out His name in the dark, dead of night,
Just to talk and to ask Him if I'm living right?
And to seek His forgiveness, to be His servant and friend,
With the hope he will balance my scales in the end.

For when it's all over, only God knows the heart,
Did goodness flow over or was it just a small part?
Each time that our faith led us on to do good,
Did our hearts warm a little, as God hoped that they would?

When God measures the weight of my faith on that day,
When the script of my life I read out, will he say,
"You did good works, my good friend, with the time that
you had,
Come in, sit and sup, and be happy! I'm glad!"

THE COMBAT ZONE

He dropped me in a combat zone,
With a chute I floated down,
Like a babe in a diaper and without a phone,
I was on my own, I found.

I bobbed and weaved, I juked and jived,
To stay beneath the fray,
But sin makes it tough to stay alive,
When arrows fly each day.

I took the flack while I grew older,
And I have some scars, I know,
But then a friend helped me grow bolder,
To stand and take the blows.

He shared God's message of love and grace,
To the lost and sinful... me,
And with faith and hope the human race,
Could find peace across the sea.

I realized that this earthly fight,

On this tiny earth, this time,
Could not be won with puny might,
It would take the power divine.

So, I gave my life to Jesus then,
Now Satan flees from me,
I have the power now, not when,
Of the One hung on that tree.

I'm at peace because I know my Lord,
Guides the steps on Earth I roam,
My armor shields me from the horde,
'Til He calls me to come home.

THE WARRIOR

It's lonely standing in the gap, the breach, the gate
unguarded.
Behind me are the weak, the poor, the hurt and
brokenhearted.
What led me here, and how, and why, when others just don't
care?
The world rushes past, indifferent, mad, I don't even rate a
stare.

Somewhere, someone is heading to a workout at a gym,
Somewhere, someone has lost it all, and lost it without Him,
Somewhere, someone will have a day with blue skies, warm
and sunny,
And somewhere, someone bet all on red, there went his hard-
earned money.

The raging storms will hit or miss, the newsmen don't
know why,
The bad guy bathes in pools of cash, the good guy's high
and dry,

The up is down, the down is up, and common sense seems
dead,
The truth is hidden deep for most in silly TikTok threads.

Rudyard penned a fact, my friend, the making of a man,
Is when those about you lose their heads, but you hold onto
yours, and stand,
Inside the gate, against all hope, deserted, left to die,
When the easy choice was to cut-and-run, without a
battle cry.

Where does my strength, my peace, resolve, come in this
mixed-up world,
When doctrine crumbles, foundations fall, when the flag of
Christ stays furled?
Think! You knew it once, you held it close, your grandma
drove it home,
With that message in the stories that she read you from that
Tome.

For, if a shred, a piece, a jot, of what I heard in church,
Is true, then Jesus is beside me now, though life seems in the
lurch.
If truth with death is better than a life that's built on lies,
That keeps me swinging the bloody blade though the Reaper's
drawing nigh.

My task is clear, I hold the line, against the legion's surge,
So those I love, around the globe, won't fall to Satan's purge.
I fight to keep the Word alive, up front, for all who'll see,
And in the end, my earthly end's of no concern to me.

For somewhere, someone is dressing up, a station wagon
waits,

To carry fresh-washed, smiling grins to church, on time, not late!
Where hope and love and faith and joy can meet youthful, fertile hearts,
They'll never really, fully know that a warrior played a part.

ON THE BATTLEMENT

God is the one and only God, though imposter "gods"
abound,
They team in realms beyond our sight, loosing chaos, fear and
hounds,
The rulers of darkness rage and surge from dawn to dusk to
dawn,
The shadows spew, the depths release, an ancient, evil spawn.

Michael sees them as they are; man sees them wearing
smiles,
Incisors nipping at our necks, while they whisper, woo and
wile.
Michael bolts the door; man lets them in to dine and share
the fire,
Whatever wares they seek to sell, we seem willing, eager
buyers.

But I wear your armor on the battlement, God, are the stone
walls high and strong?
If I'm faint or if I question, am I bad and is it wrong?
It's lonely here, it's cold and dark, before the arrows fly,

I know you're with us and for us, God, but I must ask
you, why?

Why are our numbers so sparse and few? Are we enough to
do the job?
We're just a timid handful that stands against an angry mob.
Will others join us on this wall, will others join us in the fray?
Will we live to tell our children that we failed not on this day?

From this vantage point why can't I see beyond the soft, gray
mists?
Will I lower the drawbridge by mistake, deceived by the likes
of this?
Why can't I see with second sight the war that rages on,
Between dimensions, between the realms, am I a king or just
a pawn?

Is there no hope? Are we lost and doomed?
Will we be just threads on Satan's loom?
Or will our champion rise and shine with might,
Our Lord and Master, who sets things right?

You knew us before this world was formed, you placed us
here with purpose,
We're too valuable in your scheme of things—this is no game
or circus!
Take comfort, friends, we are warriors and we'll all be home
for dinner,
We belong to Him who made us; we're no longer desperate
sinners!

So, when the walls around us tense and shake, when fatigue
and cracks appear,
When darkness tries to weasel in, replacing joy with fear,

Let's close our eyes, clutch tight our swords, back-to-back with holy spirits,
For with Jesus leading, the battle's won, we have no need to fear it!

UNFINISHED

I left so much unfinished,
So many wrongs undone,
My cupboard not replenished,
Important songs unsung.

Hurtful words I did not retract,
And wounds I did not heal.
Falsehoods, in shame, I swore as fact,
To help me make a deal.

But grievous as my overt wrongs,
That which now hurts me more,
Is bypassed service that all along,
I avoided as a chore.

A good word, good deed, a helping hand,
To one so deep in need,
Such little cost to help a man,
To plant a Jesus seed.

Yes, I left so much still on my plate,

Tomorrow would be the day,
But now it's done and now too late,
I'm no longer in the play.

If I had only paused, reflected,
My great purpose as a man,
Would have been to walk, as He expected,
To Have been my Master's hands.

THE FABRIC

The fabric of a full-lived life,
Is stained with tears of joy and strife,
The edges? Frayed, not neat and tight,
From desperate grips through stormy nights.

Its colors, faded; It's pattern, blurred,
From tragic news delivered, heard,
Some threads are loose, some breaks exist,
But, still, it's good, remember this:

You cannot mend the cloth alone,
The loom's behind you, you're not at home,
But before you toss it in despair,
The weaver waits to make repair.

That damaged cloth we sew with thread,
Can be mended only with daily bread,
With needle ready, He'll find each crease,
To make, reform, a damaged peace.

The Weaver, Sewer, Master, Friend,

Only the Savior can truly mend,
The broken, damaged, frayed and worn
Fabric, after hurt and scorn.

Please, let him make your cloth like new,
Let Him fix it through and through,
Let Him press and clean, so you can dress,
In a royal robe, not a dirty mess.

TWO SOLDIERS

Two soldiers in a foxhole cowered,
While shells, like rain, fell hour-by-hour.
Their foes across the barbed wire zone
Fixed bayonets and wrote letters home.

"When the shelling stops, they're coming, Joe,
And there's one thing that I have to know,
Is your faith in Jesus?" one soldier asked,
"You need to think and do it fast."

Joe rubbed his eyes and lit a smoke,
Was this question real or a tasteless joke?
"Sam, I never thought about it much,
Too busy living, with stuff and such.

"I don't have time to do that now,
We'll soon be dead, I can't see how
It'd do any good, all things considered,
I'll just leave this world, unsung, embittered.

"And why do you care?" Joe's voice trailed off,

He fought a tear, he choked and coughed.
"We're hopeless here in No Man's Land,
No one cares, we're dead men, Sam."

"But Jesus cares!" his mate shot back,
"And if I die when they attack,
I'll be with Him forevermore,
I'll rest on heaven's peaceful shore."

Just then, a thud fell in the hole,
A blast would soon snatch up a soul,
Without a thought, Sam dove upon it,
He looked up at Joe, at peace, he'd own it.

"Still time," Sam whispered, then he was gone,
When the thick smoke cleared, Joe all alone
Was bleeding, stunned, but still alert,
He knew that he was badly hurt.

Sam sacrificed to buy Joe time,
To grasp, by faith, without reason, rhyme,
That his mate would so gladly give up his all,
To buy moments for Joe to answer God's call.

So, in that bleak moment, with life near its end,
Joe received the Good News that was shared by his friend,
Joe struggled to get to his knees and he prayed,
And he met up with Sam on that shore that same day.

A NEW DAY

"Have I run the race?" I asked. "Have I stayed the course?
Have I shown my face, unmasked? Have I been a Christian
force?
Have I given all I have to give? Have I lifted others up?
Have I spoken truth, so others live? May I now refill my cup?"

"Well done so far, my son, so, 'yes'," God told me in a dream.
"It's time to rest and reassess, then you'll cross another
stream.
I have so much more I want from you, before I bring you
home,
You'll give new hope to many more and they'll never walk
alone."

"So, rest, but listen for my call, another season's pending.
Regain some balance, you will not fall, a fresh start is not an
ending.
Others need your gentle touch to help them find The Way.
I will chart the path before you. Tomorrow's a brand-new
day."

ON A HILL OUTSIDE OF BETHLEHEM

Two thousand years ago, this night, a battle raged, a mortal fight,
On worthless ground, two bloodied men, faced off on a hill near Bethlehem.
These two, the last, all others slain, these two, both grizzled, still remained,
With a slicing stroke it all would end, this hollow fortress—attack, defend.

Allegiance, honor, these warriors knew, they bought the lies, they drank the brew,
The marks upon their furrowed brows, forbid swords beaten into plows.
Life and death, fear, dismay, in sumptuous palaces far away,
Godless kings, demanding all, missed not the ones who had to fall.

Each eyed the other, they drew their blades, in a ring their fallen comrades made
To fight for life at the other's cost, each mourned the joy and peace they'd lost.

94

But as metal clashed, as sparks let fly, in anguish and with
muffled cry,
A miracle occurred that night that interceded in the fight.

For as one tired soldier thrust his blade, to pierce the foe that
Caesar made,
The night exploded and, in the air, great creatures gathered
not far from there.
Both soldiers stilled, let fall their gear, and together crossed
the span to near
The place where shepherds and men of light, conversed,
rejoiced that starry night.

They heard words, no, tidings, to soothe men's hearts—
hardened men, without the parts,
To show some mercy, to spare the knife, to love a neighbor, to
value life.
They received, believed, and then they knew, trust in man
alone would never do,
Consumed by those who could not taste, the poison that lays
lives to waste.

And when the angels and the shepherds left, the warrior-
hearts no longer cleft,
Were mended under silent skies, they parted before the sun
would rise.
Each found his way back to his side, changed, determined, for
anger died,
No longer foes, they were freed of sin, on a hill outside of
Bethlehem.

FORGIVENESS

For God so loved us He gave His son,
Jesus shed His blood for everyone,
For whosoever believes in Him,
Fears not the realm of Satan's den.
For Jesus leads us on His path
That steers us clear of righteous wrath,
For, though we each deserve our pain,
God's grace falls down like cleansing rain.
For God loved us first, with a love complete,
He removes the thorns that pierce our feet.
For he hides our sins from His shining face,
So we can enter His heavenly place.
And what is behind God's gracious gift?
What drives Him with His hand to lift
Us up to his throne in life, and then,
To wipe away our tears, regret and sin?
Dear friends, God's gift, and <u>our</u> gift to all,
"For–give–ness" helps us hear His call.

IN MEMORIAM

What does it mean to lay down one's life,
For friends who know peril, for friends who know strife?
But who are my friends? Are they people I know,
Just the ones that I love or should my circle grow.
To expand and include those who look just like me,
On my plot on this earth, 'neath the shade of this tree?
But what about strangers on sands far away,
Who yearn to know peace, see their children at play?
Should my gift go to babes who are yet in the wombs,
As well as those nearing the dates with their tombs?
And what if my gift, bequest and devise,
And unknown to others, should cause my demise?
And what if I love them and they don't even know?
Will they water my flowers? Will my flowers still grow?
Will they pause to remember, put tensions aside,
Will they know I gave all, my family, my bride,
My time, aspirations, my hopes and my blood,
So those that I knew not could ride out the flood?
And to those who have picnics on weekends in spring,
Would my life have mattered with the light I might bring?
What does it mean to lay down one's life?

It means loving and giving in a world that is rife,
With hatred and pain, putting others up front,
Be they mighty or weak, be they strong or a runt.
For someday, somewhere, some may stop to reflect,
What you did, that you loved them, and they'll pay due
respect.
For no love is greater, from beginning to end,
That you lay down your life, lay it down for your friend.

AT THE CROSSROAD

He said the way is narrow, but He did not say it's straight,
Or soft or smooth or paved or flat or any welcomed trait.
There are twists and turns and ups and downs along that
unlit trail,
The journey's not for the faint of heart, for they will likely
fail.

The way, the path, the road we walk in salad days of life,
May rise and fall, diverge and change, when we're visited
with strife.
The faithful one must gird for war, must toil and fight and
scratch,
The way is hard, resolve can wane, when you hit an icy patch.

We tread the way with cat-paw touch, sometimes in fading
light,
A lantern's glow, in creeping dark, fights back against the
night.
Temptation wafts and calls us toward the off-ramps bright
with glitz,

But at the stop signs, at ramps' ends, some soul-less figures sit.

Behind those figures, on-ramps await, back to the narrow track,
Some haggard travelers, who've reached the spot, surrender when attacked.
They drop their burdens and march toward where the bony fingers point,
That broad, smooth highway, down the hill, to some seedy, sorry joint.

Few will walk against the broad-road crowd, to start a brand-new day,
Fewer regain the narrow path when they've moved on, far away.
But, my friend, I beg, if a decision comes and if a crossroad looms,
Push past the one who lacks a soul, avoid impending doom.

Get right back on it, that narrow way, refreshed, you've passed a test,
The on-ramp's there for one like you, and soon you will find rest!
That way leads to where you want to be, your Father's house awaits,
With a heavy, weary, wounded soul, you'll walk upright through His gates.

THE KINGDOM OF GOD

The Kingdom of God, the Kingdom of Heaven,
Is like bread for the hungry, with or sans leaven.
It's like a drink of cool water to one anxious and parched,
And like a baby's first cry or a veteran's last march.

It's like a smile at the end of a problem resolved,
And the smell of fresh linen, when the sun gets involved.
It's like a door that swings easily and opens so wide,
That a sinner like me can fall headlong inside.

It's like the touch of a loved one, when troubles run deep,
And like the button to snooze at the short end of sleep!
It's like hearing the pleas of the poor and oppressed,
And like fitting right in no matter your dress.

It's a million warm feelings of love and of joy,
Of true peace and true patience in a girl or a boy.
It's when kindness and goodness just exude from one's heart,
It's keeping the faith when the world falls apart.

Urged to be gentle, when others are not,

Controlling oneself, when one's cool or one's hot.
God lives in the places where these sweet fruits abound,
In the spaces 'tween atoms, His Spirit is found.

His kingdom is perfect, His kingdom is pure,
It's where Truth abides always—no version du jour.
It's where light shuts out darkness, where one sheds all regret
Where one's sins are dead memories that our God will forget.

His kingdom's <u>your</u> kingdom, and you play a big part,
For the kingdom of God is His home in your heart.

EPILOGUE

One of my favorite hymns is titled, "Hymn of Promise," written by Natalie Sleeth in 1986 and published by Hope Publishing. This hymn uses examples from the natural world around us to illustrate God's promises. Nature is dynamic and evolving, but in predictable ways. Bulbs become flowers, given time and the right conditions. Seeds become fruits. Dawn follows darkness. These are facts in which we have confidence. Similarly, our understanding of God, and of His plans for our lives, become clearer the better we get to know Him and, consequently, we gain more confidence in Him. We have faith.

As we spiritually walk and talk with God, we ask questions, and we seek answers. Not everything will be clear to us for we still "see through the glass darkly," but if we persevere, if we have faith, we will see enough to believe in Him. He created perfect order in our universe. He knows how everything will play out. He is the Alpha and the Omega.

Our individual spiritual journeys are journeys of growth, much like the bulb becoming a flower. Your journey—your progress—may be fast or slow. Your journey will certainly be different from mine. You may experience peaks and valleys, starts and stops, highs and lows. We all do. You may surge forward one day and fall back the next. You may experience doubts and conflicts. That is natural. It is important that you "wrestle" with God, so that you will have confidence in your decision to commit to His will. God gave you free will, so exercise it! It's okay. God plays the long game. He is patient and He freely gives us grace according to our needs, so that none should perish.

So, talk to God. Talk to Him often. Question Him. Ask Him tough questions. Be skeptical, if you must. Just be honest and open. I think God likes a healthy debate. It lets Him know you are trying. It lets Him know you believe He exists for you would not speak to something or someone who does not exist, would you? The "Hymn of Promise" contains the phrase "...in our doubt there is believing..." If you seek, even with doubt, you will find.